A Mother's
Problem Solver

BY Verna Birkey
YOU ARE VERY SPECIAL

COMPILED BY Verna Birkey and Jeanette Turnquist
A MOTHER'S PROBLEM SOLVER

A Mother's Problem Solver

IMAGINATIVE SOLUTIONS
FOR LIFE'S EVERYDAY PROBLEMS

Compiled by

VERNA BIRKEY

and

JEANETTE TURNQUIST

Fleming H. Revell Company
Old Tappan, New Jersey

Scripture quotations not otherwise identified are based on the King James Version of the Bible.

Scripture quotations identified AMPLIFIED are from The Amplified New Testament © The Lockman Foundation 1954, 1958, and are used by permission.

Scripture quotations identified NAS are from the New American Standard Bible, Copyright © THE LOCKMAN FOUNDATION 1960, 1962, 1963, 1968, 1971, 1972, 1973, 1975 and are used by permission.

In most of the incidents shared in this book, the names have been changed.

For information on the Enriched Living Workshops taught by Verna Birkey, write: Seminar Workshops for Women, P.O. Box 3039, Kent, WA 98031.

Library of Congress Cataloging in Publication Data

Birkey, Verna.
    A mother's problem solver.

    1. Children—Management. 2. Family—Religious life.
I. Turnquist, Jeanette, joint author. II. Title.
HQ772.V479   301.42'7   78-10142
ISBN 0-8007-5050-0

Contents

PART 3
HOW WE LEARNED TO COMMUNICATE MORE EFFECTIVELY

PART 4
HOW WE ENCOURAGED A MORE ADEQUATE SELF-IMAGE THROUGH . . .

Introduction

A *Mother's Problem Solver* is a compilation of creative solutions from 140 women who have experienced a wide variety of frustrating and puzzling situations and have cried out, "Help! What do I do now?" As they sensed their lack of wisdom, they found that God does give generously of His wisdom to those who ask (*see* James 1:5).

As you start reading, you will find yourself being entertained at the antics of tots and teens and moms and dads. You will identify with nagging mornings and tantrums and food griping and jealousy and grumbling and "the TV habit."

As we face similar frustrations and challenges, we can learn much from those who have already been there before us and have found creative solutions that worked for them.

This book is an outgrowth of the meaningful sharing times at our alumnae workshops. The ones who share come from a broad spectrum of backgrounds, training, and experience, but they all have one thing in common: They have each found a workable answer to one of life's everyday problems. Our deep thanks to each workshop alumna who has shared her experience so that it can be passed on and bear fruit in the lives of multitudes of individuals and families.

Since God is a God of variety and most problems do not have just one cut-and-dried answer, we have often included several different ways people have solved the same problem.

We hope you will not just read through the book and lay it down. It can be a treasure trove of ideas and a continual encyclopedia of answers. You'll find a multitude of ideas to help you show love and acceptance to those who are dear to you. Read discerningly. Consider the principle behind each simple solution. Ask yourself, "Does this have value for me or my family? Would this deepen our relationship, enhance our communication, or bring encouragement to a sagging self-image?" And there will be creative ideas you'll want to pass on as helps to others.

Proverbs 6:20–22 (NAS) clearly implies the wonderful privileges and responsibility of parents—both mother and father—to train their children in the way they should go.

My son, observe the commandment of your father,
And do not forsake the teaching of your mother;
Bind them continually on your heart;
Tie them around your neck.
When you walk about, they will guide you;
When you sleep, they will watch over you;
And when you awake, they will talk to you.

These verses indicate that the godly training a child receives will direct, keep, and guide him in the future. What a stimulus to do what we can by God's enabling to "train up a child in the way he should go"!

You too can experience the joy of finding creative answers to your everyday problems. And ". . . if any of you lacks wisdom, let him ask of God, who gives to all men generously and without reproach, and it will be given to him" (James 1:5 NAS).

It is our prayer that this book will be spread broadly and used widely to help solve problems, answer questions, provide creative ideas, and bring new joy and gladness into family circles everywhere, resulting in greater glory to His Name.

A Mother's
Problem Solver

Part 1

How We Solved the Problem of . . .

> But if any of you lacks wisdom, let him ask of God, who gives to all men generously and without reproach, and it will be given to him.
>
> James 1:5 NAS

1

Fussing and Arguing

My TAP Chart There seemed to be quite a lot of bickering and criticism among our five children. When I stopped to consider the reason, I came to the conclusion that I was a big contributing factor. They heard constant criticism and nagging from me. Unknown to them, I began a program for myself and kept track on a chart. My goal each day was:

At least one praise or thank-you for each family member for a job well done.
A kindness shown to at least one
A loving touch for each

I realized how negative I had become in my reactions to the children when I discovered how hard I had to dig to find something good about each one. I was concentrating on their faults instead of their good points, which in turn produced more faults.

I labeled my chart *TAP* for "Touch and Praise," just in case a child noticed it. This project probably did more for me than for my children, but I did get many warm responses, and the criticism level went down.

13

Grumble Glasses   When our children were younger, we
read a story about a family in which anyone who grum-
bled would have to wear "grumble glasses." Somewhere
along the way a pair of soft plastic, funny-looking glasses
had been given to us. We used these as our "grumble
glasses."

Mom and Dad would also wear these, and it really was
a funny-looking reminder of our bad attitude which was
showing up in our words.

Even though our children are grown, we still relate to
our "grumble glasses." When my granddaughter was vis-
iting us one day and was complaining, her mother (our
daughter) said, "Sounds like we should find the 'grumble glasses.' "

Teasing   I have found that when my children start net-
tling and teasing each other, the real problem is that they
don't feel good about themselves, and they need special
encouragement. This summer I found a way of providing
that encouragement. I tack up special notes on our refrigerator, such as:

> *Lee:* I really liked the way you used a soft voice today
>   and helped "turn away wrath."
> *Tim:* Thank you for picking up all those leaves. That
>   was a big job, and I appreciated your diligence.
> *Lee:* Thank you for sharing your favorite toy with your
>   brother. That was especially kind.
> *Tim:* I especially liked the way you and your brother
>   played quietly while we had guests today. You un-
>   derstood we needed quiet talking time.

Take Off Your "Mother Suit" Our two children, eight and ten, were developing a very scolding attitude toward each other. One day Mark said scoldingly, "Debbie, get the sugar!" I quickly put on my "mother suit" and scolded back, "Mark! Ask her nicely!" He obeyed, with a subdued, "Sorry, Debbie."

Later, as I thought about it, I asked myself, "Why should I frequently be correcting their scolding with further scolding by me?" So the next time I heard Debbie scolding, "Mark! Pick up the book!" I said softly, smiling, "Debbie, will you please ask him nicely?" She blinked a couple of times and said quietly to him, "Well, will you?" He quickly obliged and even handed it to her.

After sharing this meaningful incident with my husband, he too could see areas in his relationship with the children where he could set a better example. We have both experienced more happiness as we apply the principle, "A soft answer turns away wrath."

Tattle Book Instead of running to Mother with petty grievances against each other, we had our children list these in a book. At the end of the week we went over them together. For example, Lyle wrote under Vivian's name: "She sits in the bathroom and reads when I need to use it." (We discussed the virtue of reading under a tree or in her bedroom instead!)

Often, by the time we read the book, these things had become hilarious, and we ended up laughing. It seemed to relieve the pressure of dealing with them when spirits were high.

2

Television

Controlled by TV One problem that particularly bothered me was the way our two daughters would come home from school and immediately turn on the TV. They weren't objectionable shows; it was just the control TV had over them and the time they spent at it.

I decided to try giving more of myself to them. At least twice a week I have games ready, along with a treat. I try to make the games more grown-up by using our adult games. I have found that they much prefer a game with Mommy to watching TV. It is especially thrilling to me to see they really do think I'm more interesting than TV!

TV Marbles Television was becoming a real problem in our home. Our eight-year-old daughter was getting to the point of not wanting to do anything else, and it seemed that we were having an awful lot of dissension over whether or not to turn on the TV, how long, and so forth. I was really getting tired of saying, "No, not now!" or "Please go find something else to do." My whole approach was so negative and wasn't helping at all.

We now have "TV Marbles." We have set a limit on

the number of hours of daytime and nighttime television
for each week. We have different-colored marbles to sig-
nify one-half and one-hour time allotments for day and
night. At the beginning of each week we give her all the
marbles, and she must put an appropriate one in a can
each time she watches TV. It is her choice when to watch
(programs which we have approved), but when the marbles are gone, that means no more TV that week. For
each half hour left over at the end of the week, she gets
ten cents to spend on books or records.

She has responded beautifully to this and loves the
freedom of choice this system gives her. There are no
more arguments or tears over TV at our house.

TV Versus Reading   Two years ago we felt the TV was
destroying our homelife as well as our minds. So we put
it away, and Father started reading through *The Chroni-
cles of Narnia* with the children. We would pop popcorn
and build a fire in the fireplace and make it a very special
time. We all enjoyed this special time, and eventually
the TV was sold.

The whole family is now more constructive with this
"TV time." Our time does not always work out for family
reading now, but the result of the initial project is a
closeness between the children. They read to one
another, or their father or I read to one or two children.
We are more aware of providing activities for each other,
whereas before the TV just kept the idle family member
busy while everyone else did his own thing.

What to Do When There's Nothing to Do   We have
come to realize that the television can be a very destructive force in our home. We thought for a while about

eliminating it entirely, and yet we knew that the children would go to a friend's house to watch it. More important, we were afraid that giving away our TV would be similar to running away from a problem. So we decided to try to teach control of a potentially valuable resource in our home.

We found it helpful to limit TV watching to an hour a day; however, we are flexible when there are some excellent specials. But the most important thing I've learned is that there must be an alternate plan. There must be interesting activities in the home. Mother and Daddy must be the tireless storyteller, or the TV will take our place and the stories told may not be of the quality we want.

We take a weekly trip to the library for books, tapes, and records. As a family, we read aloud from a book the children could not read themselves, trying to choose childhood classics. In addition, I keep a list that we add to constantly, called, "What to do when there's nothing to do." This monitoring system has greatly improved the quality of our life. And some days the children even forget to turn the TV on at all!

Tickets for Television With too much TV watching, I felt our children were losing creativity and learning to tune others out by tuning TV in. The children also began to realize that they did not have time for other fun things when they watched TV so much. Our solution was simple. Each child gets two TV tickets each day. Each ticket is good for a half hour. They like this system and have learned to become very selective in choosing their programs.

Our TV Chart   We solved steady television viewing this way. I put a chart on the refrigerator with each child's name and a line of minutes marked after each name. Anytime the children read a book, read their Bible, did their Sunday-school lesson, practiced music lessons, and so forth, the minutes it took were marked on the chart. Their television-viewing time could not go over the number of minutes they had logged after their names.

Each week I went over the TV-program listing and made a list of programs coming up in the week that I thought they would enjoy or benefit from and how many minutes it was. Each child could then be sure to have enough minutes logged on the chart if he wished to watch a program.

3

Jealousy

Middler Jealousy At the last workshop I attended I realized that I was favoring my two daughters over my son, twelve, who was the middle child. He teases the youngest and rides the oldest. I became aware that my yelling at him for his misdeeds was making him do it all the more.

Tearfully, for many months I prayed over the situation. I knew it would take a long time to undo years of putting him down. I began by telling him verbally that I loved him. I complimented him on his good points. I made special efforts to help him participate in sports—driving him, attending all games, praising him. Instead of nagging him to do chores, I set a time for them to be done, 6:00 P.M., and he always does them without my "encouraging"—sometimes they're done at ten to six—but they're done!

We have a new, special relationship, built over the last two years. He shares things with me and makes a real effort to seek God's help with his teasing. His relationship with the Lord has improved as our relationship improved.

21

Preparing Daughter to Accept New Baby Our only daughter would be almost two years old when our second child was due to be born. My husband and I wanted very much to make sure she accepted the baby and also continued to feel accepted herself. Realizing that a short time seems like an eternity to small children, we waited patiently until about six weeks before the due date for the biggest part of our preparation. As we went to pick out new items for our baby, we would let her choose among two or three which one we should purchase. We also shared continually with her the fact that God was giving us this new blessing, just as He had given her to us. I had prepared small gifts for her to receive while I was in the hospital—one for each day. When my husband visited me, he would then take one gift back to her, so she would know I had not forgotten her and that I still loved her very much.

Her big day finally arrived—the day she and Daddy came to the hospital to get Mommy and her brother. She was so excited to have a new baby in our home. At home she was always allowed to be Mommy's big helper. We tried never to make her feel she was an intrusion or that she was no longer needed. She was very important and very special to us, just as our new baby boy was. Our son is now two years old, and our daughter has never felt as if she has had to compete with him. We are really excited about this situation and look forward to using the same procedure very soon again, now with both of them, as our third baby is due soon!

Jealousy Over a New Father I married again after living for seven years as a widow with two little girls. My girls began to develop a bit of jealousy over my new relationship with my husband, in spite of his efforts to make them feel included and loved. It's difficult to honeymoon or be a bride and groom with four eyes and ears looking and listening! My children were fifteen and ten then.

I sensed the problem was a fear of losing the close relationship we had shared as "three girls" for so long. I determined to spend time with each child and as a threesome, so we have been taking shopping and lunch sprees. This summer I even spent a couple of times at the beach with my fifteen-year-old, who thinks getting a tan is the epitome of pleasure. I suffered the heat and sand and sunburn, but I enjoyed the reward of developing a closeness. When shopping with one of my daughters, I try to spend a little money on some special little item for her. The threat of losing my attention is gone. My girls have accepted my husband as their dad, and the honeymoon is not over!

Overcoming Jealousy Our four children range in age from fourteen to six, so of course, their choice of activities is very varied. To meet the need of everyone and to eliminate the cries of, "So-and-so always gets to do what he wants to do, and nobody ever cares about me," I planned that for eight weeks of the summer, when we were all together, each child would get two chances at choosing a favorite activity we could all do together. Beginning with the oldest, each was given an opportunity to pick an activity for the week (bowling, miniature golf, trip to the seashore, or any other favorite activity). This really helped bring harmony into our home as each one respected the others' choices.

4

Unhappy Car Trips

Squirrel Watch   I noticed each Sunday as we drove to Sunday school the family would be fussy and grumpy and rushed and hardly in a good attitude for worship. The first thing I did was to stop feeling I had to make elaborate preparations for Sunday meals. Now we have simple breakfasts, and the crockpot cooks dinner, so I myself can set the pace for a relaxed day.

One day, as we drove up the freeway entrance ramp, the kids were fussing, so I said, "Let's have a squirrel-watching contest!" Along each side of the freeway there's some agricultural land still left, and lots of ground squirrels live there. Immediately the fussing stopped and the looking began. The first person to see a squirrel got a penny. Now they just look for the fun of being first. Sometimes if it's cold or wet and squirrels are likely to be in their holes, one family member may call for a dog watch, or a bird watch instead of a squirrel watch.

We now drive to church less rushed and more prepared for worship. In addition the kids (eight and nine years old) are developing their observation skills.

25

Sing Along   When we as a family (mother, father, five-year-old son, one-and-one-half-year-old daughter) were driving in the car, everyone wanted to talk at the same time, often in a negative manner. In order to alleviate this problem, we secured a cassette tape of children's songs. Now whenever we get in the car we turn on the tape and sing—even the one-and-one-half-year-old claps her hands and smiles.

This also gives us an opportunity to share about things God is doing in our lives and the lives of others. When we get in the car, the little one instantly points to the tape and claps her hands. No more whining! Instead we are all singing praises to the Lord, and we arrive at our destination with a joyful spirit.

Traveling Projects   This past summer we took a six-week family trip from Pennsylvania to California. Our family consists of four boys and one girl, ages nine through fifteen. We planned to camp most of the way. We wanted the children to have good memories and also something tangible to remember the trip. We knew we did not have enough finances to buy souvenirs at every place we toured. We also realized that five children in a car, riding all day in crowded conditions, and huddled together in a camper at night could become frustrating to them and us. So before we departed on the trip we purchased each of the children a scrapbook. Each day they were to write, draw, crayon, or paste postcards, ticket stubs, or information folders from the places we toured that day.

We also gave each of the children a book of maps of each state, and the children enjoyed each day tracing the route we were traveling. Each day the children looked

forward to evening, when they would do their scrap-
books and map. During the day, occasionally we heard
them say, "I am going to put that on my page."

Now Riding Together Is Fun   As a family we spend a lot
of time together in our car—twenty-five minutes to
church, fifteen minutes to school, thirty minutes to the
shopping center, and so forth. My husband does much
driving in his work, so family drives are not a pleasure to
him. We rather spontaneously hit upon a way to make
this a more pleasant time for all of us. We sing!

Everyone gets a turn to pick a song. Sometimes my
husband and I sing to the children. They, in turn, sing
for us. This has proven very valuable to our family. It
eliminates the constant chatter of little ones. It checks
fighting. It draws us together into a shared activity. The
lovely words of hymns are imprinted more deeply in our
minds. And we learned that you can't sing and frown!

5

Bedtime Problems

Security at Bedtime My husband and I found that the children's bedtime was a source of great irritation to us, because we felt they took up too much of our time getting settled down and off to sleep. We discussed this and remembered that our two little girls are the most valuable possessions we have.

We began trying to "start their day" at bedtime in as pleasant, and relaxed a manner as possible. We are now trying to show more love to the girls at this time. They are responding to this more gentle bedtime manner that we exhibit, rather than the previous, "Now you get into the bed and stay!" We felt they were demonstrating insecurity, and God is helping us to correct that and give them greater security by adding more love and more patience at bedtime.

Making Bedtime Special Our daughter, Sarah, would cry very hard for several minutes at bedtime. It was an unpleasant time for all of us. After I attended the workshop, I learned how important it was that she feel especially loved at bedtime, so her good feelings would continue all night. She was not quite one year old at the time.

29

My husband and I planned a way to make bedtime very special for her. First we put her pajamas on her as a signal that bedtime is approaching. Then we take turns reading to her and we each hold her for a few minutes. After that we take her to her room and pray with her, thanking Jesus that He loves us and asking Him to watch over her during the night. Then we put her in bed with her teddy bear. She gets the biggest smile. We each give her a last kiss and close the door. At first she still cried a little, but very rarely now. If we get home later or I am especially tired and convey a hurry-up attitude, she cries quite a long time. Then I remember that it's still important to make bedtime an especially loving and peaceful time.

Talking-About-Our-Day Time My husband and I found, as most parents do, that it was difficult for our children to go to bed. There was always that last drink of water, last trip to the bathroom, and so forth. We solved this by starting what we call a talking-about-our-day time.

When the children have completed getting ready for bed—even the last trip to the bathroom, we then go to each child's room individually, and he has this time to talk about his day, to tell his father or me about anything. This has evolved into a real time of sharing, and now we all cherish this time. It is a time in which each child has an opportunity to speak privately with his father, then privately with his mother.

Many problems have been solved by early detection, and much love for one another has been expressed during this time. My husband and I now also have our own talking-about-our-day time at our bedtime. It has greatly increased communication in our home.

Tucking Them In   One time I read that the mind is most impressionable before going to sleep. So from the earliest years of my children's lives, I've tried to take advantage of that fact. I try to be sure I am always available to tuck them in bed at night (even though the methods of tucking change as they grow older). Then I sit and chat with them for a few minutes, letting them lead the conversation. I am always amazed at the subjects and thoughts that surface. Sometimes I sing to them, or we sing together. Always, I say before I leave, "Mother loves you; Daddy loves you; God loves you." They like it because it delays the sleep time!

Four-year-old at Bedtime   We were having a problem with our four-year-old daughter at bedtime. She could not go to sleep and was up and down to the bathroom and running around the room. Sometimes this caused the boys (two and six years old) not to go to sleep, even though they were in separate rooms.

I told her one night if she was not sleepy to keep her door closed tightly, and she could sit up and read with her light on—three books limit. Then she could take the responsibility to turn the light off when she was ready to sleep. She took very well to this new responsibility and was very willing to turn off her light and settle down— usually within fifteen minutes. Often before it had been an hour of various noises and trips to the bathroom.

6

Unhappy Mealtimes

Leftovers at "Mom's Place" My husband and I always enjoyed eating leftovers. However, the four children did not. I came upon the idea of "eating out at Mom's place" when the refrigerator became loaded with leftovers.

In the afternoon I made an inventory of the contents of the refrigerator and made up menus for each person. At the bottom of each menu I wrote, "The management reserves the right to limit quantities." This eliminated the problem of four people ordering the one leftover bran muffin; they simply each got on quarter of it.

That evening, when everyone was seated, I took each one's order on my pad and then filled his plate according to his order. We all enjoyed eating leftovers this way, since we each got to order from the menu what we liked to eat. The two younger boys especially like to eat at "Mom's place."

Last Call for Dinner I like to see that our table looks warm and inviting, as dinner hour is the highlight of our day. Occasionally we have candles, and I fix a pretty vase with flowers in the center of the table. However, after the careful preparation of a good dinner, I would become

frustrated, as I would call each of our four children individually, and my husband at least two or three times.
The children would stall, and my husband would visit. I
sat and looked at my beautiful table while the food grew
cold and I grew hot. I knew I had to do something to
check the resentment that was building up within me.
Then I decided to say, "Dinner time in five minutes."
When all was dished up, I called each person once, saying, "Dinner is served—last call." Only once did I sit
down and cheerfully begin eating alone. They couldn't
believe it! Now they know I mean it, and they gather
quickly at the last call.

Treasure-Hunt Supper   Family dinner time is a happy
sharing occasion most of the time. The four children eagerly tell of what happened at school. Occasionally
Daddy is away during dinner time and not home until
after they are all in bed. Dinner without Daddy sometimes becomes noisy and unhappy. The second oldest is
a boy and knows how to keep the three girls squealing.
The oldest tries to be "mother" in telling them to be
quiet.

   The last time I knew my husband would be away, I
planned a treasure-hunt supper. I wrote little notes for
each child and illustrated the youngest one's with pictures, so she wouldn't be left out. The first card had the
child's name on it and inside a poem, "In order to eat,
you can't use your feet; You'll find silverware, under a
chair."

   Then I taped a knife, fork, and spoon to the underside
of chairs in various parts of the house. A note was with
the silverware, saying where to find a glass, a note with
the glass, telling where to find the food (hot dogs), a note

where to find a small salad, and a final note for each to
bring milk or mustard or relish or ketchup. When all
found their items and food, we sat down to eat together.

It was really a surprise for them. When I rang the dinner bell and all sat down with just a note, the first question was, "Where is supper?" Then, after reading the
note, there were shouts of glee and a happy supper time
followed.

Food Gripes At dinner time we had the usual gripes
about food that various family members didn't like. I was
wondering what to do when I received a letter about
world hunger and found a small bank. So we started the
policy that anyone who makes a face or complains about
the food puts a nickel in the bank for hungry children in
the world. We have hardly collected enough to do anyone any good. If someone ever looks askance at a dish,
another child is sure to say, "Well, that sure looks like a
nickel to me."

It has made a lot of difference in the dinner-time atmosphere. We have lots of laughs and willingness to try
new dishes. And the bank is filling with willing offer-
ings.

Restaurant Game When our family eats out, we have a
game we play while waiting for our food. (You need a
napkin or paper and pen or pencil.)

The first person draws a head, then folds the napkin so
the drawing cannot be seen. The second person then
draws the body and folds the napkin; the third, the legs,
and so forth. Then the fourth person gives it a name—
usually without looking at the drawing. Then the picture
is shared, and everyone has a good laugh.

If the restaurant service is extraslow, you each take a turn doing the different parts. Even very young children can draw. Our girls are now teenagers, and we still enjoy the game.

Taste It   A good many years ago, when our children were small, I disliked the habit I saw in some homes of a family member saying at the table, "Oh, I don't like that" or "I don't want that." (Maybe they had never tasted it.) I read a suggestion which helped us in our home and became a fun thing.

When a new or not-so-familiar dish was served, we asked, "Do you want three bites (to try it) or a helping?" This worked. They were interested and learned not to pass up foods without trying them. Likes and dislikes after tasting three bites were respected.

Award for Best Manners   When our children were pre-schoolers, dinner time was spent correcting children and cleaning up spills. It was very unpleasant. I purchased a glass that had Donald Duck on it. It became the clean-place award. The child who used the best table manners and had the cleanest place around him won the privilege of using the special glass at the next meal. The kids loved winning the special award. The table was cleaner, and dinner became a pleasant meal.

Dinner Conversation   Often our dinner hour was less than tranquil. For some reason, we parents seemed to use this time for correction and accusation of our captive audience. Strangely, our children's appetites were never very good, but reappeared miraculously as soon as they left the table! I saw this happening, but seemed unable to stop it.

Then I began to jot down ideas during the day of funny or interesting topics we could discuss together while eating. I listened for items on the radio or TV, or stories told by friends, or something from magazines or newspapers. Now, although it doesn't work 100 percent of the time, our conversation at the table is pleasant and conducive to good digestion.

"I Don't Like This!" My children are all grown now, but I remember that at mealtime one child might decide he didn't like something he had chosen to put on his plate. Without making any fuss one way or the other, I'd let it go. In most instances it was an attention getter. However, I would be sure to remember the food. When I prepared it again and that child would ask for it, I would calmly remind him that he'd better not have it because he "didn't like it." After serving this two or three times in this manner, I finally let him try it again without any fuss.

It was amazing how little fuss ever was made over meals. Today all my children like a wide variety of foods. It worked for me! And I had four children.

Best for the Family I belong to a birthday club, eight women getting together for a potluck dinner. It is my turn, once a year to have it in my home. I clean house extraspecial, set the table with a lace tablecloth, good dishes, my best silverware, candles, and flowers. It looks very nice.

One evening when it was my turn, my two boys, ages ten and twelve, came in and one said, "Oh, Mom, why

can't we have dinner like this?" I began to reflect on our
dinner time. My husband sits in his lounge chair in front
of the TV. The boys sit at the kitchen counter, and I
sometimes even stand on the other side to eat. No one
eats together. What a shame! Why not the best for my
family every day. God spoke to me that day.

7

Our Fretful, Fearful Daughter

She was such a happy, sensitive little rascal—so excited! School was everything that she'd hoped it would be, and more. And the fun of running down the path with her older sister to catch the big, yellow school bus made her whiz through her morning chores.

At about 1:00 P.M. she would come running into the yard and in the door, eager to inform me of each exciting detail of her morning class.

About this time a friend brought his old television to my husband to tinker with and repair. After fixing it up, Jack brought it in the house for us to use so he could test it for a few weeks. Since we had had no TV of our own, it was pretty exciting to go in, turn the button, and be entertained. Carol began going in each day after our chats and watching TV, while I busied myself at household chores.

Before a week had passed, Carol began asking me to drive her to school. She complained of tummy aches daily and began to cry and fret. The ride home on the bus became a trauma. At the thought of the "long, noisy, and lonely" bus ride she would sob uncontrollably.

My husband and I became more and more concerned.

39

We asked the driver if she knew of anything that had
happened on the bus that might have scared her. No, she
knew of nothing. We talked to Carol. We prayed with her
each evening. We read Scriptures of God's care and love.
Still she sobbed at the slightest thing. She became tearful and afraid of our leaving her bedside at night. We
talked to her kindergarten teacher. She couldn't figure
anything out. We talked to the school psychologist, and
she spoke to Carol. All she could get out of her was that
she felt "scared inside."

Jack and I were so troubled and hurting so badly inside for Carol. It was a burden that we continually
brought before the Lord, with tears. Whatever happened to our bouncy, happy little gal we had nicknamed
Tigger (after Winnie the Pooh's friend)?

After an exceptionally hard day for Carol, Jack and I
went to the Lord, earnestly begging for His wisdom and
recommitting our little one to Him, claiming His prom-
ise in 2 Timothy 1:12: ". . . I am [positively] persuaded
that He is able to guard and keep that which has been
entrusted to me [Carol] and which I have committed [to
Him] [Carol], until that day" (AMPLIFIED).

The next day, while I was sitting at my sewing
machine, I heard the familiar sobbing. There was Carol,
sitting in front of the TV, crying. I slipped my arms
around her. "Alice is going blind, Mama." It was as
though a light flashed on in my mind. She had been
burdened down so heavily by her daily viewing of the
soap operas. I recalled what a psychologist friend of ours
had said several years earlier: 90 percent of the de-
pressed, restless women who came to him watched the
soap operas faithfully.

I quickly flipped off the TV, and I prayed right there

with Carol, thanking Jesus for His wisdom and praying that God would mend her little overburdened heart and mind.

Immediately I began on a campaign to fill her mind with "whatsoever things are true, honest, pure, lovely, and of good report" as Philippians 4:8 says. I gave her verses to memorize. In fact, we began to "feed" all of our children a verse of Scripture each morning, as regularly as they ate their breakfast.

It was several weeks before we saw marked improvement. But we did see it. After a while she was back riding the bus cautiously. Now she's back to bounding in the back door—bubbly and full of a blow-by-blow account of her happy day!

I truly believe in the power of the Word of God in healing our little one's mind.

8

Other Problems

Stay in Your Own Bed!   When our son was two and one-half years old, he was getting out of bed every night and coming in bed with us. At first we didn't mind, but it did make our double bed crowded, and my husband decided he shouldn't be forming this habit. However, Nathan kept coming in two and three times a night. We were getting exhausted!

We talked it over with Nathan, but he really didn't know why he liked our bed so much. We considered insecurity problems. We talked to our nursery-school instructor and a child-behavior instructor at adult night school. Meantime he was continuing to come in two or three times each night.

For fun one day I took Nathan shopping for a new bedspread. We decided on a heavy quilt lined with blue flannel. Lo and behold! The first night he had the quilt he slept through the whole night! My husband and I were surprised, but didn't say a word. The next night he slept through also! Finally we said, "Nathan, we are so proud of you for being such a big boy and sleeping in your own bed all night."

He answered, "I love my bed now because I don't get cold anymore!"

Potty Training   Our two-year-old granddaughter was at the potty-training age, and everything had become quite confusing. One day I hit on the idea of setting the stove timer for every two hours. I thought perhaps this would help her set the habit of becoming conscious that she might have to go to the bathroom. She thought this was very special! She began to listen for the timer to go off. Then she would run to her potty chair. She soon found there were no more uncomfortable diapers, and the reward was the privilege of wearing training panties. Needless to say, pressure for both the child and the parents was off.

Fear of Death   We had three deaths in our family within one year, through heart attack, heart surgery, and cancer. Our three girls lost a grandmother, a grandfather who lived with us, and an uncle. We had openly shared during devotions or fellowship at dinner about death and our relationship with the Lord. By all outward appearances all seemed well with our three girls—at that time twelve, nine, and eight in age. Then a problem began to spring up at school with our youngest. Although it seemed physical in nature, we finally discerned that it was a fear and withdrawal because of the deaths.

   We worked out a plan with her teachers, just between ourselves. At lunch, recess, or any free time, she would be allowed to call home to see for herself that I was indeed alive and well. In the morning I would carefully share with her my activity schedule for the day, so she would know when to call. Her next oldest sister would be permitted by teachers to visit during the day and chat about homework or go to the bathroom with her. These visits were kept short. I would also write notes or draw funny pictures to put in her lunch box.

Eventually we were able to phase out these things. Now only occasionally when Art and I go away by ourselves, Holly feels threatened, so we do take up one of them again, like the note in the lunch box.

Security-Blanket Graduation Day Lori's father promised her a party when she would give up her nighttime security blanket. He said Lori could choose the day. A few weeks ago she chose the day. We had a cake, balloons, presents, and a festive family dinner using china, crystal, and "the works." It made her feel very special. It was a growing-up milestone in her life. We reassured her of our love for her, God's love, and that because of this she did not need her blanket anymore.

Left Out Being new in our neighborhood, the children were experiencing some feelings of being "left out," especially our two- and four-year-old boys, who could not go to school with the others.

One morning as I prepared ahead of time for the new day, I packed each of them a special sack lunch and tucked in extra goodies—marshmallows. They were most pleased. By 9:00 A.M. they were outdoors with sack in hand, but were immediately confronted by two neighborhood children who zipped by on their bicycles saying. "We can't play with you. We're bicycling today."

I heard my four-year-old try to entice their attention with marshmallows. But their response was, "We have gum." Immediately I was confronted with two pitiful broken spirits saying, "They won't play with us. Can't we have gum, too?"

Knowing that gum would not really solve the problem, I wondered what I could do. Then the Lord helped me think of a creative plan to help my little ones feel loved and included. I went to the closet and produced a large old quilt, took the children out on the front lawn, and spread it out for a picnic. This drew the immediate attention of the two neighborhood children. I called for them to come share a special picnic with marshmallows. They were there in a minute. A very rejecting experience was healed, and friendships had begun.

A Five-Year-Old and Death   One of the hardest moments in my life was to convey to my oldest son, who is five now, that God is love and heaven is a happy place. After my husband's sudden, accidental death one year ago, my little boy and I missed Daddy very much. My other two children were too young to understand. With God's help I explained that Daddy was happy and got to sing to Jesus every day, all day long.

Of course, there have been many tears, but when we say our prayers at night, we thank God that Daddy is happy and can sing all the time. But it doesn't end there. We talk about the day when Jesus will come back and take us Home! Some days Todd will say, "When is Jesus coming?" What an opportunity to convey hope!

Change of Schools   Our family had to move from California to Texas on very short notice. Our children, ages five, seven, eight, and fourteen, had grown up in our California home. Each child was experiencing problems with change of school and friends and had a poor attitude toward this new life.

One day I decided to take each child separately to the town's cafeteria, let him choose what he wished to eat and spend one hour alone with him, letting him talk of anything he wanted. As the children got out of school at different hours, it worked very well.

By the end of that day, the cashier of the cafeteria stopped me and wanted to know what was going on! The children's attitude started to change. They grew to love Texas, and our relationship grew even closer than before.

Thumb-sucking Our four-year-old son sucked his thumb at bedtime and naps. I knew he was aware that he could give up thumb-sucking if he wanted to. So I provided an incentive.

He had been asking for a certain toy he had seen in the store. I asked him if he would be willing to give up sucking his thumb to get it. He said, "Yes." So we talked about making a calendar to put on his door. For one week we could mark off each day that he did not suck his thumb. He thought that would be fine.

The first night he failed, but I told him, "That's okay. It was just an accident. You can try harder the next time." From then on he has had very few accidents, and he would even voluntarily tell me about these. He also loved to cross off the days as they went by. Some days he would cross them out before he went to bed—expecting victory!

That week ended his thumb-sucking, and it was not traumatic. I felt his secret of success was first, motivation, then, no punishment for failure and no pressure.

Part 2

How We Taught
Our Children
to Take Responsibility
for . . .

*Train up a child in the way he should go: and
when he is old, he will not depart from it*
Proverbs 22:6

9

Getting Up and Ready in the Mornings

Ten Cents for Bread We had frustrating mornings in getting David off to school. He was so slow getting downstairs that he usually had only five minutes left to eat breakfast, brush his teeth, and gather his books together before the bus arrived. I was exhausted by the time he left—constantly urging him to hurry, getting his meal ticket for him, reminding him to take his trumpet.

One day I realized that I was not helping him in this way or teaching him responsibility. I had an idea, but first I discussed it with his teacher. She agreed. This was our plan. I would call him earlier each morning, allowing him more time to get ready. I would no longer remind him of his meal ticket, and so forth. If he forgot, his teacher would give him ten cents—enough to buy a piece of bread at lunchtime, so he would not starve!

I discussed the new plan with him before we inaugurated it. He thought it was great. He worked out his own way to help himself. He gets his books ready the night before, and he's out waiting for the bus five minutes

51

early. And never once did he have to eat just bread for lunch!

Alarm Clock   Our oldest daughter is fourteen, our son, thirteen. We found that every morning we were going round and round trying to get breakfast over and get them ready for school—not saying anything about first getting them out of bed! After talking it over a number of times, we finally decided to get them each an alarm clock and make them fully responsible to get up and ready in time. (I knew it would never work!)

Would you believe, the very first morning they had thirty minutes to relax before leaving for school! And it has been that way for the past three months. They are much happier when they leave—for a number of different reasons:

They don't hear me yell at them
It does them good to feel they can really do something on their own
They have enough time now, so they enjoy doing little things for me before they leave

Nag, Nag—Hurry, Hurry   Ricky was very poky in getting ready for school. It was always nag, nag, nag—hurry, hurry, hurry. Then when we heard the bus coming, we became frantic, fearing we'd have to go out of our way to take him to school, or worse yet—that he'd be left home! So we hurriedly stuffed him into his snowsuit and shoved him out the door, holding our breaths for fear the bus wouldn't wait long enough. This left us exhausted and him bewildered. It was time for a change! It wasn't a good beginning for any of us.

Friday I began telling Ricky of a new plan we would begin on Monday. The plan was that he would be responsible for himself—dressing, eating, brushing teeth, combing hair, getting snowsuit on, and going out the door at eight o'clock. I would not say one word. If he was unsuccessful and missed the bus he would spend the day in bed—no visitors, no TV, no playing. He accepted this responsibility miraculously well! Now he's up and dressed at 7:00 A.M. with breakfast eaten by 7:30 and ready by 7:45. He has not missed a day in three weeks—and without one word from his daddy or me.

Nora's Surprise Can   Our daughter had trouble in the mornings, keeping her mind on what she was supposed to accomplish. She was not deliberately being disobedient, but she was very easily distracted. I found myself nagging her constantly, and I became very frustrated. My husband and I talked about the situation and came up with a surprisingly workable solution.

We decorated a coffee can and called it Nora's Surprise Can. Then we explained that each morning she got downstairs, dressed and with her bed made, by 7:00 A.M. she could open her Surprise Can. She has been the first of our three children ready for school ever since.

Some surprises include: a stick of gum, a note saying, "I love you," Lifesavers, a nickel, a new pencil, a jelly bean, a gum drop, and so forth. After three months she herself suggested that she didn't need the can anymore!

Things-I-Do-for-Myself Chart   As a single parent, things can become overwhelming at times. I find that I begin to nag and criticize in a destructive manner. The results are apathy, discouragement, and more for Mom to do because cooperation drops to zero. So, beginning with my youngest, who is six, I made a chart of specific things she was to do for herself each morning and evening, as well as one chore in the house. That is, in the morning she was to dress herself, brush her teeth, eat breakfast, and gather her things for school. This got me ahead of nagging, and I found I was praising her for doing things in a grown-up way. Although I had to take time to plan with her the steps each day, I had more free time to get things done before I left for work, because she was no longer waiting until I nagged her to do each step. It was great.

Contented in the Morning   I discovered that the way I send my children to school is very important. What are their thoughts as they're leaving? Are they happy and content? Angry or sad? Can't wait to get away? Before my daughter goes to kindergarten, I sit down with her and read her a story. I hold her in my lap. I tell her I love her and that I will miss her. I watch her from the door as she goes to our neighbor's for a ride to school. I call out, "Good-bye! Have a nice day!" It brings me pleasure to see her walk out the door happy.

Memory Verses   While my three daughters are preparing their lunches, I choose two or three Scripture verses and write out several questions relating to them. This takes about fifteen minutes to prepare. Then we spend twenty minutes or so reading the Scripture and answering and discussing the questions. We have opportunity to discuss things that would not come up in day-to-day conversations. This has been a priceless part of our day. My oldest daughter has shared, "This is something I don't want to miss!"

Good-Morning Song My parents sang a very happy good-morning song to me every day. My husband and I began to sing it to our son before he could walk. Our son is two and a half years old now. Every morning he greets us with "Morning, happy day, Mommy and Daddy." A few weeks ago Grandma and Grandpa were at our house for lunch. Peter, our son, went around the table asking, "Grandpa happy?" "Mama happy?" "Grandma happy?" They were so pleased to know that their singing has made him aware of others' happiness.

10

Doing Family Chores

Responsible for Puppy My ten-year-old daughter wants a puppy for companionship. As a single working parent, I do not want more responsibility, so I challenged her with ways to show me her willingness to care and be responsible for a puppy on her own. If she could do the things I listed for six months, without constant reminders, I would let her have a puppy.

She has done an excellent job—and with a joyful attitude—keeping her room neat, helping with chores at home, and being a real help to me. I now feel I can trust her to take care of a pet. In addition she has learned the joys of earning and of sharing in maintaining a home.

Creative Helpfulness Our thirteen-year-old son is very faithful in following through on responsibilities that he is specifically given. However, my husband and I wanted to find a positive way to help him become more sensitive to ways he can be helpful or show love to other members of our family without always first being told.

We decided to draw a monthly chart. Every day, for one month, Ron was to think of and do something helpful for someone else in our family. Each day it had to be something different. There are two other children, a dog, my husband, and I—so he had plenty of room to be creative. We encouraged him to pray each day over the unique way God wanted him to help another. He would then record on his chart whatever he had done for that day.

The mail came in unexpectedly from the mailbox, the dog was taken out for exercise, the living room was vacuumed, his things were picked up in his room more frequently, stories were read to our three-year-old, and so forth. It was exciting!

The end result was as we had hoped—a habit was formed, and Ron continued to be sensitive to dishes that could be washed, time to be shared with younger children in the family, and so on. The reward was his choice of a restaurant where we could all go out to eat. That was a great celebration for all.

Cinderella   When we were young, my mother would play Cinderella with us on Saturdays. In the morning we shared household cleaning jobs, but twelve noon was the deadline. We would turn into a Cinderella by cleaning up and dressing up. She always had a special place for us all to go.

As my sisters and I grew up, we continued this practice and would treat ourselves to something special on Saturday afternoon or evening. Now our two sons help me on Saturday with household jobs plus washing cars and yard work, but we always finish by noon. Tonight we plan to go to the boat show.

Camp Planning   When our two girls were four and five years old, I decided to get their opinion of how to celebrate Father's Day. My idea for this was two-fold. I wanted them to feel included in the decisions and planning, as well as teach them some basics on preparing and detailed planning.

Their choice was to go camping at a nearby lake. They got paper out, and together we made lists of food and equipment. Although they were under school age, I spelled the words for them as we decided on menus and needs. The camp-out was a great success and has become a yearly outing for Father's Day.

Last June they were in grades one and two, and I noticed how they had developed in planning. Each girl was given a different meal to figure out and on her own, list everything needed.

Give Them Time One most helpful thing to me is to give another person (child or friend) time to respond to certain situations. For example, when a child has to do something he doesn't want to do or doesn't like to do, such as go to the dentist or have a special speech class, assure him you know he doesn't like it, **and** it is going to be hard. Then give him time to accept it. Support him with understanding instead of arguing or demanding, "This is just the way it is! You are going to have to do it!"

I have found that if I try to understand children's feelings and encourage them, this eliminates a lot of problems of authority—the power struggle. I've seen the negative attitude change to a positive one when they sense my support and understanding. I have also found this true with friends when plans are changed or new situations come up. If I don't judge their first response right away, but give them time to adjust or rethink, this eliminates a lot of conflict and misunderstanding. Give time and allow them freedom.

Mission Possible   Sometimes we have extra chores for our children to do when they return from school. Rather than telling them, or nagging them into doing it, I have written them a little note such as, "Mission possible. Welcome home, Scott. Your mission is to clean up the patio after you have a snack. This note will self-destruct when put in the wastebasket. Love, Mom."

No Reminders From Mom   Our sixteen-year-old daughter, Loretta, had a messy room and sloppy personal habits. One day in conference with her we decided:

> I won't nag her to clean her room and bathroom and pick up after herself around the house.
> I won't clean her room anymore—no cleaning sinks and mirrors, no vacuuming, dusting, and so forth
> I won't wash her clothes
> In order to do any outside activities at school or with friends, she will have to assume responsibility for these items without any reminders from me

The room became a complete mess for three weeks; it was completely unlivable. Loretta had more dirty dishes in there than were in the kitchen! Clothes were left where thrown and weren't washed, so she had to wear them dirty and wrinkled—including a uniform for her part-time job.

Then one day she wanted to go with some friends for pizza, and we denied her permission. Suddenly she started washing—five loads. It took till two-thirty that morning! Her room and bathroom are slowly appearing a

little better. We have a long way to go, but now we're
moving in the right direction.

Make-Your-Bed Week When our children were in
elementary school, I tried to teach them good habits
such as making their beds, cleaning up their room and so
on, but it seemed as though I was constantly nagging
them. One day I decided that we would concentrate on
only one habit per week. So I made a sign and put it on
our bulletin board in the kitchen. It read, THIS IS
HANG-UP-YOUR-COAT WEEK. Or, THIS IS MAKE-YOUR-
BED WEEK. They thought it was fun. They would even
run to look on Monday to see what the new sign said.
And it was much more effective than Mother's nagging.

Comparing Rooms To encourage our children to make
their beds, we said that their rooms had to be as neat as
ours. So it has become a fun project—comparing rooms
with Mom and Dad's. If Mom and Dad don't make their
bed before school, they can't say anything to the children if they don't. Our eight-year-old daughter likes to
check Mommy and Daddy's room!

Chore Coupons by Mom Our three children, ages four,
seven, and eight all have certain chores and responsibilities which they are expected to accomplish each
day. So that I don't have to constantly remind them, we
have a chart indicating what they are to do. There are
occasional grumblings, but they generally do their share.
One day, for no special occasion, I gave them each a
coupon book. These coupons contain a chore to be done
by Mom. So if they have a day when they don't want to
make their bed, or do some other chore, they present that

coupon, and I do it for them gladly. They were delighted and have even made special coupons for me to use in return.

Chore List from Dad My husband is generally not home on Saturdays, when the children are home from school. The responsibility for weekly chores fell on my shoulders. I found it difficult to keep our children on track as far as accomplishing the items their father told them to do. They would try to keep from finishing their work by telling me that Dad didn't say this or that. It became an area of contention every week. I would get so upset by being put in the middle every Saturday, that I would end up angry at my husband for leaving me responsible for all of this.

I finally shared my frustration with my husband. He came upon a solution that really works for our family. He now gets up early enough on Saturday to take a few minutes to write them a note on which he lists their chores for the day. He might do something like this: "Clean out garage; take a ride on bike; hoe one row of peas; play catch with a friend; read John 15:1–8; memorize 15:1; take out garbage."

At the end of the list he tells them when he will be home, so they know when the chores are to be finished, and also a reward that will be theirs if everything on the list is checked off. Sometimes, the night before, my husband will ask me for suggestions for meaningful projects and possible rewards.

When the children complete each item on the list, they check it off. When they begin to argue with me about the justice of a chore, I don't have to be the warden; I just say to them, "Call your father and share with him your reasons for not doing the chore." (He is accessible by phone.) Sometimes they call, sometimes they go ahead and do the chore because their only reason that time is laziness!

The Disappearing Box When our three children were small, I was continually nagging them to pick up their things and put them away. My husband was a student, and we lived in a small home, so this kind of orderliness was necessary just to be able to walk through the rooms! The more I'd nag, the more the problem seemed to escalate.

I decided the most important time for the order was when my husband came home around five, and again before the children were to go to bed. So the Disappearing Box became a tool to cut down on nagging. I made one suggestion to the children that it was time to pick up. Then I gave them a reasonable amount of time to finish what they were doing and clean things up. Things that were found lying around after that were quietly put in the Disappearing Box, where they remained until the end of the week.

A favorite toy was sorely missed for a few days, but a lesson was learned on the responsibility of caring for their belongings. This also included Mom and Dad, and sometimes it took real discipline on Mother's part when tempted to get a pair of shoes from the Disappearing Box before Saturday. If we found the same item in the box several weeks in succession, it would have to be bought back with pennies from their allowance.

Four-Year-Old Responsibility When our son was about four years old, we had problems with him concerning

certain responsibilities we felt he was capable of handling. However, he didn't want to handle them most of
the time. So we made a star chart for him. Since he could
not read, we drew pictures to remind him of what we
expected of him. A high chair was to remind him we
expected him to sit till the end of each meal. A pair of
glasses reminded him to wear his glasses the required
amount of time, a toy box to pick up toys, and so on.

We rewarded him with a star for each category when it
was fulfilled for that day. We set a goal of ten stars for his
first big reward, which was a trip to the library. Later
there was a trip to the zoo. Recently, when we cleaned
Billy's room, we found his star chart and reminisced
about how young he had been, how well he had done,
and the good times we had had.

Game of Chores   One thing my husband has done for
our two sons, ages seven and nine, is to make each of
them a chore game. On a big piece of paper he drew a
path divided into spaces, with a start and a finish. As they
do particular chores and /or thoughtful deeds around the
house, they get to color in spaces accordingly. As they
get to certain places along the way, they get little rewards (ice-cream cone at the ice-cream store, and so on).
Then at the end they get a bigger reward—zoo, library,
or some other outing. It has really worked to give them
incentives to accomplish things.

Make It Fun   One way that I have used to make working more fun for the children is to make up slips of paper
with a job written on each. These are usually small jobs
that aren't time consuming, given according to age and
ability. Each slip is pulled out, read, and completed be-

fore choosing another slip, until all the jobs are finished.

I'm not sure what makes the difference, but my children have come to me and asked if I would write "slips" for them. They want to help, and they enjoy this method. It's proved to be a peaceable and fun way to get the jobs done without the nagging! They know they're responsible for getting all those slips out of the way.

Fourteen Stars We have two girls, three and six years old. In order to encourage them to begin to accept responsibility in our home, my husband and I have set up a reward system. It works this way. Each of the girls has four or five specific jobs to do each day, given according to their age and capability. Each girl makes her bed, brushes her teeth, and gets dressed before breakfast. Then one girl's special duties may be to feed the cat, empty the cat's water dish and refill it, and maintain a specific area where toys are kept.

This has had a profound effect on our girls. Even the three-year-old is making her own bed (after a fashion). The six-year-old asks for additional jobs. Why? The reward is a chart with a star given for each day when all the jobs are completed without any mention by my husband or me. At the end of fourteen stars, the children are taken to our local Christian supply shop and given their choice within a certain limit. Sometimes they even choose gifts for my husband and me. I nag less and am enjoying their positive attitude toward responsibility.

11

Managing Their Money

The Twenty-five Cent Special   As a family fun time, we go to a shopping mall and give each family member twenty-five or fifty cents, as finances allow. Then we turn the children loose, with a designated period of time in which to return to a special meeting place. They are each to find the "best buy" for the twenty-five or fifty cents. When the time has elapsed, we gather with our buys and keep them secret until we have gone to a special place, such as an ice-cream parlor, where each family member unveils his twenty-five- or fifty-cent special. We then vote to see who has found the best buy.

This has proved to be much fun and a good, inexpensive evening with the family, teaching them the value of shopping for the best buy.

Making the Money Last   On our vacation from California to Canada last summer, we had our two teenage children, fifteen and eighteen, keep track of the expenses of the trip. Before we left, we met and planned our budget—specifically how much was needed for gas, food, lodging, and entertainment each day. We planned

67

together our route and stopovers. The children did all of the bookwork. We bought a travel diary, and they kept records of every expense every day. Halfway through our trip, because the kids had economized and put us in inexpensive motels several times, they figured out we had enough for a few nights in a luxury motel, which was a real treat.

It made such a relaxed atmosphere for my husband. He didn't even have to think about making the money last, because the children were very aware of —in fact, felt in charge of—how much we could spend on food, horseback riding, canoe trips, or whatever. When we came home, we had money left over, and we told them that they had done a good job of management! We used some of the leftover money to pay for developing the many pictures we had taken.

We did this two years ago on a trip to Yellowstone, when the children were sixteen and thirteen. These are valuable learning experiences for them, as they now know how much is involved in paying for such a family trip.

Earning, but Learning To earn Christmas money, my daughter, age eleven, and I made a learning-responsibility chart. This listed jobs, other than her regular chores, for which she would receive ten cents each time she thought to do them. If I had to ask her to do it, it did not count. The purpose of the chart was not only for earning money, but also to help her to notice things around the house that needed doing.

She was very responsible and earned enough money to buy Christmas gifts of her own choosing. She felt very good about spending her own money on other members of the family.

Austerity Program We wanted to take a trip West but didn't have the finances available. My husband suggested we go on an austerity program. We asked the children—ages five, seven, eight and ten—what they would be willing to do. They wholeheartedly gave ideas such as, "Ice cream only once a week." "Use plastic bags 'over' to pack lunches." "No snack foods such as chips, and so forth." "Make our shoes last longer." They very graciously did these things without complaining, because we had a goal. We took the trip, and everyone thoroughly enjoyed it. It could have become irksome if we had demanded that they give up some things to take a family trip.

When we left that morning and had gone about one-fourth of a mile, our eight-year-old asked, with a twinkle in her eye, "Are we off the austerity program?"

Five Cents a Bed Being a working, single parent of boys seven and four years old, I have had problems in knowing how to motivate them to help with household tasks—particularly repetitive ones such as making lunches, taking out garbage, and making beds. I also needed to teach the value of money, as our means are limited. The Lord graciously showed me an idea this spring when my seven-year-old wanted a baseball mitt.

I made a chart assigning certain monetary values to certain jobs: five cents, empty wastebaskets; five cents, load and start washer; ten cents, sort and put away dry laundry; five cents, make bed; twenty-five cents, drag out trash cans early Wednesday morning; fifteen cents, make lunch; twenty-five cents, do dinner dishes. I also made a chart showing the value of the baseball mitt (seven dollars) in five-cent increments. As each job is done, we mark off the amount earned. He has the immediate reward of seeing more money earned, but no money is paid until the whole thing is earned.

12

Being Courteous

Playing House   I am a grandmother now, but when our two daughters were small, I was a very young mother and wanted so badly to do a good job of mothering. This idea came to me.

I spent an hour each week with the girls playing "house." We used that hour to practice "growing up." One of the girls would go outside and ring the doorbell, the other daughter and I would go to the door, greet her, invite her in, take her coat and put it in the closet, offer her tea or coffee, and sit down and visit. We also practiced introductions, answering the telephone, giving directions, and so many of the little things that make growing up easier.

The girls have children of their own now, but they still tell me how much those hours together meant to them.

Please and Thank You   When I brought my newborn home from the hospital, I determined to be courteous with him. As I changed his diaper, I would say, "Please lift your feet, Eric." Then I'd say, "Thank you." It has been very gratifying to hear him say "please," "thank

71

you," or "excuse me" to adults and to his baby sister. He is now four; she is two.

A Mother's Foresight Our family was Lancaster County, Pennsylvania, farmers and, as such, kept very busy. Our mother, knowing someday we would be off the farm, in other situations, tried to have a special type of meal at least once every two weeks.

For example, one time it would be a buffet. We would practice and learn the methods for buffets. Another time it would be a formal-dinner setting—learning to use the silver properly, the courtesies of being seated, and so on.

We did not appreciate then the hard work of learning how to dress appropriately and have good manners but now as a school teacher off the farm, how much I appreciate her foresight. This was especially interesting if we had a house full of cousins to share the evening with us. Our home always seemed full of cousins, and they, too, benefited from our mother's teaching.

Courtesy Time As a means of helping our girls, ages four and seven, learn better table manners, my husband made up a list of good manners to be practiced at the table. This was put into a frame and placed close by the table, so it could be referred to at each dinner time. Each item that was practiced, such as putting napkin in lap, offering food to one another, and so forth was worth one minute of time with a possibility of earning twenty-five minutes of time each week. Then on Friday night or Saturday each girl could choose one parent with whom she could spend the earned minutes privately, to do anything she wanted to do without interruption. The girls love the special times and look forward to their "courtesy time" each weekend.

Manner-Improvement Project We felt a real need to have better table manners and general courtesy at the evening dinner table. So my husband wrote up a list of essentials such as:

Respond immediately to the dinner-is-ready call
Hands washed and hair combed
Sit properly with napkin neatly on lap
After grace, pass food in an unhurried manner
No one eats before Dad or Mom (this was used as a basic guideline in waiting till each was served)
Wait until everyone is through before asking to be excused

Then he said that each week one person would earn a dollar for the best performance. It was interesting to see how the children responded to this, especially at the end of the week when Daddy didn't remember to mention who won the dollar! They were also very aware of one another's infractions. It became a real fun family improvement project. It was especially fun for them when they realized Dad or Mom did the best!

Table Courtesy It was my bad habit to constantly remind the family of ways they needed to change. Because of this constant harping, they never seemed to remember what I had told them. It was a source of irritation to me at dinner time when I had cleared the table and served dessert, that the family would begin eating their dessert the moment it was set before them. By the time I sat down to enjoy my dessert, they were ready to be excused.

One Sunday, before bringing in the dessert, I asked if they preferred a sermon or an object lesson. Of course they all preferred an object lesson. So without saying anything I fixed only my dessert, sat down and began to eat it. They all looked bewildered. Finally one asked, "Where's ours?" I just kept on enjoying my dessert. Finally one of the children said, "Okay, I guess we need the explanation, too." Once again I told them they were always to wait until the hostess began eating before they were to eat. To this day, whether at home, or away, the members of our family observe this courtesy, and will often remark in private that certain guests needed either a sermon or an object lesson.

Please One day our five-year-old son was asked to change the channel on the TV. After he had done what was asked of him, he turned around to his father and said, "No one ever says *please* or *thank you* to me. You say it to Mommy, but you never say, 'Please turn the channel, Kevin. Thank you, Kevin.'" From then on we purposed to say *please* and *thank you* to our children.

13

Cooking

Strictly From Scratch   To encourage our girls in cooking, I told them if they made the rolls (or the cake, or pie), the least I could do was the cleanup. And it worked.

Our girls are twenty-one and nineteen, and both are great cooks. We're missionaries in Africa, and cooking is strictly from scratch, so there's been a lot of cleanup work, but it's been worth it down through the years. Wouldn't *you* like to cook if someone cleaned up *your* mess?

Praise Spurred Them On   As a way of encouraging responsibility, my husband suggested we give our girls one day each week for helping prepare the meals. They could choose what they would like for breakfast and dinner. I would be sure all the necessary ingredients were on hand and be available for whatever help they needed. It really worked well. We had varied, interesting meals, and the praise each received spurred them on to plan for the next week's meal. They learned new recipes and gained confidence in their cooking ability. It was delightful for me as a mother to see what they could do, because I hadn't been given that responsibility as a girl.

Later, one girl asked to have the opportunity to make all the breakfasts, as she had the latter part of her day occupied with baby-sitting, studies, and so forth. While she got breakfast, it gave me opportunity to spend time in the Word each day—a good start in the day for me!

Tasty Creations Preparing meals has never been my favorite thing to do. Many times after I had planned and prepared what I thought was a great meal, someone would be dissatisfied. So I decided to give everyone an opportunity to help plan and prepare the evening meal. Our two girls, ages nine and six, help by taking turns planning and making the salad or dessert. (I give assistance when needed.) As they share in putting together the meal every night, they have really become creative and enjoy helping. Dad also helps by adding his praise for their willingness, their special effort, and their tasty creations!

Daughter-Sized Jobs When my eight-year-old daughter would desire to help with dinner, I would give her a mother-sized job to do. Of course, I would often have to stand and wait for her to finish her part. Impatient as I was, I usually took her job over. Now, as God has opened my eyes, I'm engaged in rebuilding that self-confidence I so carelessly destroyed. When she comes to help me, I:

   Assign a task not critical to the sequence of meal preparation
   Allow plenty of time for her to finish
   Give better instructions and demonstrate, remembering that it is easy for me, but new for her
   Assign less to do (example, cut a few carrots, not all)

14

Personal Needs

Calendar for Teens After school I would expect the children to do certain jobs, but it seemed as though they always had mountains of homework to do and had no time to help me. My husband came up with the idea of a calendar for each week. We use a notebook, and for each child, for each day of the week, we note things like music lessons, a test coming up, a party, or whatever. Because my husband goes over the weekly schedule at the dinner table, I now know exactly what each one has facing him or her, and I can give more. I also know better how much they can help me. They can see exactly where they stand and can start studying for a Friday test early in the week, instead of the night before.

Now they will often come to me and say, "Mom, I don't have anything coming up tomorrow; what can I help you with?" Since we all know each other's schedule, I find the children asking each other how the test was, or when they need to leave for certain activities—they have more interest in each other. Another bonus: better grades, because they are studying for tests earlier!

The Sad Lunch Box When she started school, our daughter, Mary Beth, had a problem remembering to take her lunch with her when she got off the bus at school. Several times she also left her empty lunch box on the bus in the evening, so the next day I had to pack her lunch in a paper bag. I decided that to help her remember, I would write a letter-reminder on the bag, but of course she was too young to read. So I drew a sad face with tears coming out of the eyes and a big frown. Then in a "balloon" I wrote how the lunch box felt— cold, lonely and afraid of the dark—when she forgot it on the bus. After two of these lunch-box faces, she didn't forget anymore.

Anxious to Be Independent Our son, Dan, a college student who is working this semester to earn money to return to school, was anxious to get an apartment of his own, so he could "learn responsibility" and not be "dependent." He really could not afford to do this and still meet his college expenses.

My first reaction was to try to talk him out of it by reasoning. Then I decided that would be doing what he most feared—making decisions for him. I told him I would pray while he was looking for a place. Meanwhile I backed off and tried to check my own spiritual need and anxieties. I tried to give him as much independence as I could by doing only the laundry he left in the hamper—not going in to pick up what I thought needed to be washed. If he was late for a meal, I left dinner on the stove with a note to help himself.

What happened? Well, he hasn't left home, and I have enjoyed his company. Yet we are both looking forward to his going away to school again next semester. He is proud of the money he's saved. He has been voluntarily more helpful, and communication between Dan and my husband and me has been delightful.

Calendar for Tots While teaching kindergarten at a Christian day school, I was impressed with the novel way one mother taught her son responsibility. Since he often couldn't remember what day to bring his tennis shoes, and so on, she made a little calendar for the week. Instead of words, she pasted pictures of the articles he was to take to school that day. He would check his calendar and get the needed articles for his book bag. Then he was ready for his day.

15

Obeying

Tantrums My four-year-old was going through a period of screaming and tantrums. When he couldn't open a door, it would set off a real siren inside him, and the arms and legs would start kicking and hitting. My tendency was to lose control myself and then discipline the child, but I was not gaining at all in that way. Even after the discipline, the child still had tantrums when he couldn't open a door or find a book, or other article. Then one day I discovered that a calm conversation opened the way to a simple and lasting solution.

He needed to learn how to control himself, even though he was very young, and he had to begin to ask for what he wanted! So I explained to him, "I would be glad to help you open the door, but you need to come and ask for help saying, 'Please help me open the door, I can't get it open.' Otherwise I won't know what you want." After this, when a situation arose, I would wait nearby to see what he would do.

The next day I was in the kitchen and heard some crying in the bedroom. Then it quickly stopped! Our four-year-old walked into the kitchen and said, "I can't

81

get the drawer open, please help me." What a victory! He had remembered that it would not help to cry. The answer was to ask for help. That was a victory!

Rules for Discipline   We decided that the rules in our house weren't clearly defined, so we sat down with our son and talked about what rules we needed, trying not to have too many. We wrote them down. We then discussed discipline with him, coming to an agreement of what was fair. Then we wrote that down. This was hung in his room. Now when he breaks a rule, he calls to my attention what should follow. This also keeps us from disciplining unfairly, and he feels secure. As he looked at some of the consequences, which he had agreed upon, he said, "Wow! I'll never break that rule, Mom!"

Time-Out for Attention   In the three years since we adopted Mike (our oldest of four children), there have been many problems and struggles. Mike had been severely abused, both physically and mentally, and was very strongly programmed into negative behavior. My husband and I have struggled with Mike and his many problems, trying everything we knew.

Several months ago, the Lord led us to a friend at church who helped us work out a program for him. When Mike does something negative—lying, fighting, destroying something—he goes for a time-out. He sets the timer for five minutes and sits in the bathroom until the timer goes off. Then when he does something positive, we're sure to praise him and notice it. At the end of the day, if Mike has less than four time-outs, he gets to stay up a half hour longer—a time we spend with just him alone so he gets lots of individual attention. If he has more than four time-outs, he goes to bed a half hour earlier. Those half hours are important to Mike, and he's really changed his behavior.

Short on Order and Discipline   As a new Christian family with five children, we were in some ways short on order and discipline. The children ranged in age from one to thirteen. Knowing we needed to establish some new, desirable habits to make a more orderly and happy home, and being a very busy and forgetful mother, I made a list of rules and posted them prominently. This helped me to remember what was now going to be expected, and it was also a constant reminder to the children. The poster consisted of about ten things, such as:

Knock on the bathroom door
No running in the house
Come to dinner when you are called
Ask to be excused before leaving the table
Don't play in the street

Looking back these sixteen years, I realize that it really did achieve what was intended, to a large degree. There was more authority in that poster than I could have achieved as a very harried mother trying to remember what was written on it. It was a very successful method of training.

Overreacting and Overcorrecting   My husband and I were having a problem with overreacting to things the children may have done during the day, then overcorrecting them. We sat down and made some rules for ourselves and discussed them with our three children.

We would set fair limits and let the children clearly
   know what they were.
We would quietly discuss with the child any behavior
   we did not like.
We would discuss the discipline involved if this behavior continued.
We would always hug and love each other after correction, to clear the air.
We would pray together before we go on to the next
   thing.

This has made a remarkable change in the atmosphere
of our home.

The Bean System   When our daughter was three years
old, I began to feel that all I did was spank her! Yet I
knew she needed discipline. Finally I heard about the
bean system. When Janet did a job or duty around the
house, I gave her one pinto bean in her special jar. (One
bean for emptying the trash from the bathroom to
kitchen, two beans for making her bed alone, one bean if
I helped, two beans if she picked up her brother's toys,
one bean if she picked her own up, and so on). When
Janet had four beans, she got a penny. When she would
not obey or did something she knew she shouldn't, a
bean was taken away.

When Janet has one or two pennies, she can go with
me to the store and buy whatever she wants. She usually
buys candy and gum. Janet is five now, and the beans
have helped in three ways:

She has learned to save money—she now waits till she
   has five or ten cents.
She has learned a simple concept of math. She counts

the beans till she gets four, and then she has a penny. She also counts her pennies.

Although she is still spanked for saying no to me or any intentional disobedience, she is spanked much less.

Now occasionally I say, "Looks as though I'll have to take a bean away," and she hurries to do the job.

Rebellious and Wounded When our oldest child was very young, my husband and I felt that we must discipline him at each infraction of rules or crossing of the wills. We spanked him ten or more times a day, with the formal ritual and all. Then the Lord began showing us how rebellious and wounded in spirit he was, and how much more he needed love and healing than extreme discipline.

We began studying in the Scriptures what God is like as our Father. We discovered a part of His nature that we had been almost totally ignoring as parents. We saw that God's nature is to be so loving and accepting and forgiving, and He is not as concerned with seeing that we get what we deserve as making sure we see what he's trying to teach us. So we felt, as parents, the need to be like Him to our son—loving, relaxed, and waiting for his readiness to learn the lesson.

We have been able to say to him, "When you run out of love or feel jealous, please come and tell us. We will find time to help you and give you love." He does that frequently, before doing things he used to do to get our attention. We have had to spend lots of time trying to mend his spirit, so deeply wounded from our harshness in the past. God is helping him internally! He is definitely independently responding to the Lord.

Moping After Discipline When our children mis-
behave and have to be disciplined, we have noticed a
lingering anger, manifested through a moping attitude.
The child is not yet convicted to seek God's forgiveness.
Instead of pressing him to ask forgiveness when we
know he is not ready, we tell him that we love him, then
we refuse to let him dwell on the situation. We put him
to work doing something short, yet helpful regarding the
family unit. For example, we assign ten to fifteen minutes of cracking walnuts, weeding a garden or baking
prerolled, frozen cookie dough. His obedience to complete the task takes his thoughts off of self and invariably
changes his entire attitude.

As the assignment is completed, we make a special
point of praising him for a job well done. The entire
attitude of the home changes. Later in the evening, before bedtime, we pray individually with each child. By
that time the perspective has changed, the situation can
be objectively discussed, and forgiveness among family
members and in the sight of God can be reinforced.

A Future in Sing Sing! Most children occasionally take
things that don't belong to them. I had already handled
this problem successfully with our first child, so I pur-
sued the same solution with Timmy, our second. One
day he came home eating a candy bar he had not paid for.
I explained that things must be paid for, and we made a
trip back to the store. I escorted the child in with money
in his hand. We explained that the money was for the
candy bar already consumed.

With Timmy my fail-safe plan didn't work! Things got
worse. He would take money from my purse to buy toys
from neighborhood children. I had to leave him in the

car when I went in stores. Finally, I lost control and did what all the books say not to do. I likened him to Al Capone and predicted a future in Sing Sing. My poor, trembling six-year-old!

After calming down, but still being desperate for a solution, I suggested he and I look in one of Mommy's many child-rearing books. Since he didn't know why he stole, and I didn't know, maybe a book would. We opened a book and the first sentence was, "Some children steal because they don't feel loved."

I turned to Timmy in shock and with tears in my eyes said, "Why, Tim, you know Mommy loves you, don't you?" He began to cry and we hugged and kissed and comforted each other.

He never took anything again. Later he told his second-grade teacher, "I used to take things when I was little, but I don't anymore!"

Attitudes Reflected I peeked around the corner and saw my three-year-old spanking her Baby Tenderlove on its bare bottom. Wishing to know what her "baby" had done to merit such a severe chastening, I asked her, "Why are you spanking baby?" "Why," she said, pausing quite some time to think, "Well, because I love her . . . ."

By jotting these little things into my personal book (called *Out of the Mouths of Babes*), I learn what kind of messages my four little ones are receiving from my words and actions.

Part 3

How We Learned
to Communicate
More Effectively

> *Let no unwholesome word proceed from your mouth, but only such a word as is good for edification according to the need of the moment, that it may give grace to those who hear. And do not grieve the Holy Spirit of God, by whom you were sealed for the day of redemption. Let all bitterness and wrath and anger and clamor and slander be put away from you, along with all malice. And be kind to one another, tender-hearted, forgiving each other, just as God in Christ also has forgiven you.*
>
> Ephesians 4:29–32 NAS

16

Designing Projects to Enhance Communication

Bread-Box Communications We help keep family communications open with a bread box! Eight years ago our oldest daughter and family left the states to live in England. We all had little time for letter writing, but with a family at home and family abroad we wanted to keep the family together.

I had a Tupperware bread box. The idea came, "Why not fill it with little, inexpensive gifts for our daughter and family?" They were delighted! Our daughter said that every time the bread box came, it was a holiday. She also returned it with small gifts, and we were all excited when it arrived.

Our son is in service now, and we have a bread box going back and forth with him. It helps keep the family communications open, as we express our love through the bread box.

Family Communication Center On a large four-foot-by-six-foot bulletin board in our family room we dis-

play the children's artwork, school papers, special messages to one another, encouragement, congratulations,
happy-birthday cards, verses of Scripture, and pictures
clipped from magazines. This is really a family communication center. (But it's not the one by the phone for
dental appointments!)

This display area gives each family member a space to
show his achievements, share a message, and display his
talents. It's the family place, not Mother's bulletin board.
Sometimes we work together for a special seasonal
display—children love to cut, paste, plan, arrange.
Sometimes we all (except one) work secretly to provide a
special surprise for one member, letting him know how
special he is to us.

This area is really near the center of activity in our
family. It gives us all a sense of belonging in our home.

TNT   At least once a week my husband and I sit down
and write each other a love letter. The purpose of this is
to verbalize to each other the love and appreciation we
feel, and which often goes unsaid or is just assumed.

A very important part of the letter for us is to share a
TNT—The Nicest Thing. We tell each other what we
think was the nicest thing the other has done or said, and
how that has made us feel. Sometimes those TNTs are as
powerful as dynamite! And knowing how my husband
feels about the things I do for him tends to encourage me
even more to do nice things just for him.

Communicating Love   We were having communication
problems with our teenagers because of some damaging
attitudes we have had towards them. In order to help

mend this buildup of hurts, I recently put a blackboard in the kitchen, where we write messages. Through the months we have been writing messages of love and approval to each of the children. Our sixteen-year-old daughter has used the blackboard to write some of her real feelings and expressions of love towards us, in response to our doing this for her. She is becoming much more loving and is more easily able to communicate verbally.

We are all slowly learning what real love is. The blackboard helped us begin to express our love when it was difficult for all of us to express love verbally.

Communicating Love   One evening we gave our teens the project of writing down evidences that they felt loved by their parents. They were to include our attitudes that they caught, our actions that they saw, and our words that they heard. Then we wrote down what we are saying and doing to communicate love to them. Then we compared notes by discussion and tried to discover: "Are we loving so our loving is heard?" "Are our love signals caught?"

Avoid Arguments   Right after our marriage, my husband and I decided to try to avoid the arguments that often occur when little habits appear that irritate the other partner (socks on the floor, coats on chairs, and so on). We each made a list of four things we found most annoying in each other's habits. Each time one was committed, we awarded five points toward our next word-game session. Instead of nagging and fighting, we laughed and had fun. The point accumulation was also a good incentive to take time to relax and play our word game. With both of us working, we needed to take relaxation time.

We have never had a disagreement over habits, and the habits disappear eventually. I heartily recommend this to all!

17

Open Sharing

Handling Hurt Feelings   Recently I took what my husband said to me in a completely wrong way—as a "put down." So the rest of the evening I was not myself; I was hurt and confused. He noticed, of course, but didn't know what he had done or said; so to clear the air, I brought it up. After talking it out, we realized it had merely been miscommunication.

We decided that next time that happens, the one who has been offended should say, "Could you rephrase that last comment? I think I have misunderstood." We should also assume the best. When we hear something confusing from the other, just remember, "He/she would never do anything to intentionally hurt me."

Heart-to-Heart   My husband and I were both feeling the "poor me's." I was being mean and felt sorry for myself. Just before he left for the worship service, I said to him, "You are getting so hard to live with!" Good timing! He even told the elders he couldn't do his part in the meeting that night. When he came home, he said, "I might as well have stayed home!"

While he was gone, I read some verses: "An excellent wife, who can find? For her worth is far above jewels. The heart of her husband trusts in her, And he will have no lack of gain. She does him good and not evil All the days of her life" (Proverbs 31:10–12 NAS). "An excellent wife is the crown of her husband, But she who shames him is as rottenness in his bones" (Proverbs 12:4 NAS). "The wise woman builds her house, But the foolish tears it down with her own hands" (Proverbs 14:1 NAS).

Well, by the time he came home from Sunday-night worship service, I was a broken woman. I shared these things, and we talked heart-to-heart for many hours. We realized all over again how important it is to talk things out, sharing what we're thinking and how we feel. Since then I try to read over these verses and apply them to my life every day. It certainly removes the black, sad, and heavy heart!

Real Soul Communication   Just this week my husband and I had real soul communication. We each openly shared several things we'd like to see changed. During our discussions I had to pray two or three times that I would not take personal offense, but accept in love what my husband was telling me in love.

He wanted three things to be done: no dishes after his arrival home, the door to be unlocked around the time he would be home, and fifteen to thirty minutes to himself when he first gets home. After I thought about his requests, I realized what simple and easy things they are. If they will make his life more pleasant and our relationship more satisfying, then I will make every effort to do them.

Sharing Happenings of the Day   Our oldest son would never talk about his day at school. When I asked him about his day, his reply was always, "Okay." Then one day I realized that when I tell him what I do during that day he opens up and tells me about his day. Now it is really interesting to hear him talk about his school day.

18

Removing Barriers to Communication

Creative Communication With Turtles   Since my oldest boy was a complete turtle, always in his shell, I decided to find a creative way to communicate. I tried confronting him first thing after school with a drill, "What did you do today?" "Did you have fun?" Only to be met with "yes" or "no," and most of the time silence.

After much prayer, this thought occurred to me. The one thing he is really interested in is trucks. So off to the library I went to find out all I could about trucks. When my son came home from school that day, I met him with information on the Peterbilt out of Detroit. "Did you notice the size of the engine?" was his answer. From then on he has shared so much with me, that sometimes, I wish he'd go back into his shell just long enough to give my ears a rest! (Not really!) Praise the Lord that I've learned from the workshops to take an interest in his interest.

Lack of Communication   For twenty-five years of marriage, we had nothing but unhappiness, and yet I didn't

know why. My husband and I had the poorest relationship and virtually no communication. Every time I tried
to converse with him, after a few sentences he would
storm off in anger, and I would sit trying to figure out,
"What did I do? What did I say?" I was so unaware of
my faults that I could never find the reason for his actions.

Through the workshops I began to realize that maybe
the fault lay with me, not him. I began to pray as David
did in the Psalms, "Lord, reveal to me my secret faults."
Then my eyes began to open to the fact that I was damaging our relationship by my attitudes.
I came across to him as:

"I always think of it," making him feel incompetent
"I'm always right," which slammed shut the conversa-
    tion
"I already knew it," which made him feel inferior and
    stupid
"I have the best way," which lowered his self-esteem

Now that God has revealed these things to me, and I'm
beginning to correct them, you wouldn't believe the
change in the relationship and communication between
us. We are even discussing spiritual matters, and he was
never interested before.

Go and Play—I'm Too Busy   My husband and I have a
two-year-old boy, Donny, and a one-year-old girl, Karla.
Our little girl entertains herself quite a bit of the day, but
our two-year-old wants to be involved in what's going
on. He loves to help with dishes and vacuuming and to
have me read to him. One day I overheard him playing,

and he was asking his "pretend" mother a question. Then he answered for her, "Go and play—I'm too busy."

Well, the shock of hearing him say that made me realize how often I had said that to him. I suddenly saw that though the words were different, I was actually saying to him, "Go away. You're not important to me." It brought tears to my eyes and conviction to my heart! This was not what God wanted me to communicate to my children. They need to know that I love them and will spend time with them.

Now because of these new insights and patience that God has given me, when Donny asks me to read, I ask him, "When we are finished will you help me pick up toys?" He eagerly and joyfully agrees. Our days are much happier, and my relationship with my children is growing in joy.

Admitting Wrong   My husband and I realized we both came from homes where our parents were "never wrong." We thought parents had to stand their ground or "lose face" to their children. We decided to review the effects this had on us and to think about the effect of these attitudes on our children. We discovered the fact that if parents are never wrong, then no opportunity to forgive ever arises. Consequently resentments build between all family members, and the result is unhappiness for all. My husband and I decided we would muster our courage and admit to our children our wrong actions and reactions. It took great courage for us.

I had the first opportunity. I had screamed at my son for misplacing the car keys when I was ready to go on an errand. Then I discovered that he really hadn't misplaced them. I had! I took my tearful, resentful ten-year-old aside and told him I was wrong. I asked him to forgive me. He stood there in amazement. Then out came the resentment bottled up in his short life. I agreed with him. He was absolutely correct about my past errors. I was amazed at the things he remembered. After he had released his pain, he put his arms around me and said, "Mom, you do love me. I forgive you." We both cried with a joy and a love for each other that was never there before.

My husband had his opportunity also to repair and restore love to his children by admitting his wrong. Our children have learned to forgive each other and themselves, because God taught us it isn't terrible for a parent to tell his children when he is wrong.

Jumping to Conclusions   A failure of mine is to jump to conclusions in what has been said, not really listening to what the child is communicating.

My daughter in high school asked if she could drop her Spanish class. My immediate reaction was, "No, why should you drop a class?" And there was no more discussion! She honored my wish and completed the quarter. After that she never took another Spanish course, although a previous teacher had said she should be encouraged to become an exchange student because of her command of the language. I found out later that two-thirds of the class had dropped the Spanish class because of the teacher's attitude.

If I could do it over, I would honestly question her to find out why she wanted to do what she had asked. Hindsight is slowly teaching me not to jump to conclusions.

Oh, Never Mind!   I am outspoken and opinionated and have found this difficult to overcome. Often without realizing what I am doing, I will respond to my children in a harsh, strong voice. When they had just begun to share some experience from school, I have heard each of the four of them respond with, "Oh, never mind," and walk away. Recognizing that I have been exhibiting a relation-damaging attitude, and causing them to feel defeated, I have been working to restore their confidence in me.

One thing I have tried to do is share an activity separately with each child, even when inconvenient to me. For example, I attend high-school football games to watch the band one daughter plays in. It has been my prayer that God will make my present actions speak at least as loudly as my past words.

19

Learning to Listen

Special Attention   When our son Mark was quite small, I used to sit by his bed and listen to his prayers. After he was finished, he would talk to me, many times discussing problems, sometimes expressing joys and successes. Later, when years passed, the door to his bedroom seemed always to be closed. He became a secret person. Fifteen is a difficult age for children, and it is perplexing to mothers—especially to me. He was our fourth child.

One night when he was in bed, ready to go to sleep, he asked me if I would rub his head. As I sat quietly by his bed listening, I found it wasn't so much the headache as it was a need to have help with a problem.

Now we both know when he says, "Mother, will you rub my head a moment?" he is really saying, "I need your help or your advice, but please don't make me feel I'm asking for your help. You really know I can solve it. I just thought I'd let you know how I'm going to do it." We have a good relationship, open communication, and respect for each other's opinion, although we don't always agree. He has the freedom to be himself and to learn through failure. And so do I.

105

Conscious Listening   Most of our married life, I had
tried to encourage my husband to share himself with me.
My manner was forceful, and it did not work; he would
withhold himself even more. I wanted so much to have a
deep relationship with him, but I didn't know what to
do. He just would not share!

Finally, through the workshops and a friend, the Lord
pointed out to me my need to listen. I knew this was a
real weakness in my life, and I really wanted to change.
What a battle though! It has become a conscious effort to
keep my mouth shut and really be quiet and let my husband share—if he wants to. No more pressure!

Eventually, he started opening up and sharing—first a
little, then more and more. Our relationship has grown
so much deeper, and we are growing as persons. He tells
me how much he appreciates how I listen now, and how
he feels so free to share himself with me! I have to constantly give my attention to this, but it's so worthwhile.
It's helped my husband gain confidence in sharing with
others, and it's helped me in other relationships as well.

"Mom, You Never Listen!"   My seventeen-year-old son
had repeatedly told me, "Mom, you never listen!" I
couldn't see what he was talking about, so I passed it off
as "just his age." I always listened to him. He gradually
talked to me less and less, and then he no longer con-
fided in me at all. This bothered me. I couldn't figure out
why, but concluded it was due to our poor job of bringing him up before we had a change of life through Christ
a few years ago.

Last year my sister stayed with us for two weeks. In a
sharing time one day she told me I needed to learn to

"actually" listen. She told a story she had read about "active" listening. It made sense! So I decided to try it. Gradually, little by little, I began to see that I had not been listening to my son or to anyone else. I had been listening with one ear, but thinking of all the advice the person needed, or why they shouldn't think and feel the way they do, or how I understood because I had gone through it before also!

As I began to see it, I realized I needed to first listen quietly—keep my mouth shut, in other words—then to acknowledge their feelings and thoughts, perhaps repeating them back to them in other words without jumping in with advice. Well, my son has been talking to me more lately. He even tells me where he is sometimes. It's not perfect yet, but it's encouraging to see even a little progress, knowing more will come. What a reward for learning to really listen!

Thumbs Up, Thumbs Down Sometime during our third year of marriage (we have reached six and a half), my husband Brian and I decided we weren't happy with the way we were responding to each other during conflicts. After a lengthy discussion, we decided that part of the reason was that usually one or the other was not ready to listen at that point.

We decided to use a signal. "Thumbs up" means, "Okay, you can talk to me now, and I will hear what you are saying." "Thumbs down" means, "Anything you say to me now will only fall on deaf ears. Try again later." It has really worked for us, and we have each learned a little patience from this activity.

Part 4

How We Encouraged a More Adequate Self-Image Through . . .

Therefore encourage one another, and build up one another, just as you also are doing . . . . And we urge you . . . encourage the fainthearted, help the weak, be patient with all men.

1 Thessalonians 5:11, 14 NAS

20

Commendation and Praise

Not *Bad* Girls In October last year we adopted two girls, ages four and nine. We soon came to realize that both girls had very low self-images. They thought that they were *bad* girls. So my husband and I decided to leave the word *bad* out of our vocabulary. First of all we would pick out one thing each day to praise the girls for. When they did something wrong, we would say, "That was not good." Then we would talk about the problem. We have found that just sitting and talking about the problem with them makes them feel better. And we have noticed over a short period of time that they are already showing signs of liking themselves more.

Schoolwork Packet Each Monday our son brings home a packet of papers which he has completed in school the week before. These are to be signed by the parents and returned to the teacher the next day. When he brings home this packet, my husband or I or, better yet, both of us together, sit down with him and go over each sheet of paper individually. This accomplishes a two-fold purpose. It helps him feel that these efforts on his part are

recognized and important. We make a special effort to
commend him on his hard work and to encourage him
where he has difficulties. The second purpose ac-
complished is that it alerts us to areas in which he needs
special help at home. Our son eagerly awaits this time. It
is a special time, just for him, when he is given center
stage and we pay particular attention to his accomplish-
ments and needs in school.

A Lovely Smile   Our two-year-old son had a very seri-
ous nature. Although I enjoyed his personality, I knew
that for social development it would help him if he
smiled more. The Lord reminded me that it is possible to
develop someone's weak areas through positive reinforcement. So, whenever he smiled, I would say, "You
have a lovely smile." My husband joined me in com-
mending him. We have noticed a marked difference.

Now he's three, and he laughs and smiles often. If we
had repeatedly said, "Why don't you ever smile?" the
effect would have been quite different, we're sure.

Praise and Smiles   As a parent with the desire to train
my children, I spent many years concentrating on watching for error in their ways and then correcting them verbally with a firm tone of voice or a wooden spoon on
their bottoms. Finally God made me aware of the vital
part that praise and smiling play in building a good self-
image and how much more readily we respond to praise
than criticism. It required real mental effort on my part
to watch for the many nice things the children did and to
compliment or praise them.

I asked God to cover the many errors I had made in
training and to strengthen me and give me wisdom in the

area of praise. How faithful is our God! I now find great joy in watching all four of my children ages seventeen, nineteen, twenty-one and twenty-four bound together in a deep love and respect for one another.

Encouraging Son's Appearance I try to give frequent encouragement to my son, Steve, concerning his clothing. I might say, "Steve, you look so sharp today—your colors look so good together." He especially loves to dress up for church. Then he comes up to me and asks, "Mom, do I look sharp?" I say, "Boy, you sure do," and his five-year-old face just lights up.

21

Recognition

Another Badge, Please Our six-year-old daughter, being the second child, has needed special attention to make her feel as competent and useful as her brother. When she helps me with several parts of housework, she receives a Mommy's-good-helper badge, made of paper. She wears it proudly and shows it to friends. I hadn't realized this would be so helpful, until she showed it off, treasured it, and volunteered more help several weeks later in order to receive, "Another badge, please." Her peers were impressed.

World's Greatest Dad There was a joke at our house about our older boy's teams never receiving any trophies, while our younger boy received a trophy just for being on a team. Every time it was mentioned, my husband would jokingly add, "And I never won a trophy in my life, either."

So for Father's Day this year my boys and I had a trophy made with "World's Greatest Dad" engraved on it. After his first surprise was over, he said, "Now I'll probably never get another trophy." For our anniversary in July, I had a trophy made up with the engraving, "Happy Fifteenth Anniversary. I love you. Sally." Both trophies are in a prominent spot in the living room now—placed there by my husband. I think he feels like a winner!

Top-of-the-Tree-Award   A classroom activity I enjoyed as a kindergarten teacher began at Christmastime with a triangular tree on the bulletin board. Each child's name was placed in a slit on the tree. One day someone did a particularly loving act. Very spontaneously I said, so all could hear, "Heather, I'm going to put your name on the top of the Christmas tree!" From then on I used that recognition as a reward for a kind or loving act: comforting another child who was frightened of having a shot, giving up a treat when there was not enough to go around, assisting to pick up a spill of Legos or pegs.

That tree was still on the bulletin board at Valentine's Day, and I was actively watching for ways to reward children whose names had not climbed the tree regularly.

Recognition for Schoolwork   We reward and give our children recognition for their schoolwork. Every two weeks, on payday, I sit down with each child individually and go over her previous two weeks' papers, which she has been saving in a folder on my desk. We discuss and evaluate each paper, and a value is written on it. After all the papers have been reviewed, she picks out the one she is most proud of, and it is hung on the wall or on the refrigerator. The money value is added up, and payment is made. When she gets her "pay," she puts 10 percent away for the Lord. One half of what is left goes to savings, and the other half goes in her pocket.

This has been very effective in encouraging pride in their work. They especially enjoy the special attention, and they are learning some basics of money management.

22

Emphasizing the Positive

Favorite Pants Are Too Small   One day my three-year-old had picked out a favorite pair of pants to wear. She had outgrown them, and they were several inches too short. A friend stopped by, and I was embarrassed by the way Lucy looked. I explained, jokingly, "You know how this age likes to pick out their own clothes. Sometimes they don't know how to put things together, do they?"

As soon as I spoke, Lucy became very quiet. When my friend left, I immediately went to Lucy and asked if I had hurt her feelings by what I had said about her pants. She said, "Yes," in a very soft-spoken but hurt way that really tore at my heart.

I realized how self-centered I had been in thinking only about what other people think of me, instead of giving her my full support. I asked her forgiveness, and she gave it gladly.

She still proudly chooses her outfit for the day and we are gradually working on better judgment in her choices.

Why Didn't You . . . ?   I never give my fourteen-year-old daughter enough credit. I always find some-

119

thing wrong with everything she does. When she cleans her room, I don't compliment her on her good dusting or sweeping, I only say, "Why didn't you empty the waste can?" If she washes dishes I only say, "Why didn't you clean the stove?" If she has a good report card, I say, "You can do even better than that!"

I'm training myself to comment on all that she does do right—which is an awful lot!

Tears and a Wounded Spirit As a mother I know I have made many mistakes. You never really know just how many until they are all grown up. Perhaps this recent one would be a good example. Over a period of time I was encouraging my thirteen-year-old not to eat so much. We had talked about her complexion and her weight, and she sincerely wanted to "work at it."

One day, as she came happily in after school, she asked if she could have a piece of cake for a snack. Instead of carefully advising, I said sarcastically, "How much did you say you weighed?" Needless to say there were tears, and a wounded spirit that could not be quickly mended.

Encouragement Notebook When I realized my son needed more positive reinforcement, I started a little notebook which I kept on my desk in the kitchen. Each day I wrote in it one or two positive things I saw him do the day before. I also wrote thank-you's and apologies in it. Each morning as he ate breakfast he would reach for that notebook and read what I had written. If it was something good he had done for me the day before, you could see him planning at breakfast the good deed he would do, even before he went to school. What I wrote each day seemed to be an encouragement to him to do more of the same.

On Valentine's Day I told him I would like to give him something, but didn't know what. He can't have sugar, and he's too old for toys. Around that time I had been remiss in keeping up his notebook. So he said, "I know what you can do—write in my notebook!"

"That's Just Like You!" One thing I have started to say is, "That's just like you!" in an encouraging, positive way. For example, when my eight-year-old daughter deferred to a friend in a matter of "turn taking," allowing the friend the first turn, a chance came a few minutes later for me to take Ellen aside and say, "That was just like you, honey, to let Miriam have the first turn."

There are many occasions each day when I find I can positively affirm someone by saying, "That was just like you to . . . ." Obviously this could be misused, "That was just like you to forget to pick up your socks, again." But obviously that's not the right idea!

23

Communicating Love and Specialness

Her Special Day One of the most valuable things I learned from the workshop two years ago was to look very closely to find the specific interests or talents of each of our children. We now take special time with each one at least once a month for what we call special days—days on which that specific child has one of us (either my husband or me) totally for the whole day, all alone without sister or brother.

This has paid off handsomely, especially with our middle child, the only girl. She is frail physically and has now had to have her activities curtailed. Both brothers are very athletic, but the Lord has blessed her with a great deal of interest in the arts. Her special days are spent at museums and concerts. She told me just yesterday that she knew God loved her, because He gave her a mommy and daddy who loved to do "her" things with her, and that she was glad her brothers were so good at sports! We are so pleased there is no envy here!

123

Little Notes for Lunch When I packed lunch for a child who had a low self-esteem, I would write a short, to-the-point note on his napkin. I always wrote the name of the child and then a short message such as: "I love you!" "Smile, we love you!" A smiling face and "When you think, don't forget to think again." "Bring homework home, please." "See you soon." "Mom loves you; Jesus loves you." "We care! Work hard!" "What would you like for supper?" "How does fishing sound after school?" "Be kind, help a friend." "Be careful! We love you!"

Treated as a Lady From the earliest times I can remember, my father always treated me as a lady. He opened the car door for me, let me go first, and ordered from the menu for me. This always made me feel so valuable. He still does, too! I'm thirty-three.

Our Baby Story When our daughter was born, four years ago, a friend gave me the idea of keeping a diary of her first year, month by month. I incorporated all the pictures we had taken and made a story, as if she were writing it. As she grew older, my husband read the story of her first year to her. She loved to listen and look at the pictures. This album has been very good for building her self-image and helping her to know how much she is loved and wanted. It also makes for a special time between daddy and daughter.

Projects of Love Before our daughter goes to sleep at night, we have made it a frequent practice to list the people who love her. She enjoys this, and it builds positive attitudes toward herself and others.

I also made up a song about my daughter. I try to add a

verse each year. In it I include what her name means. In the verse I add each year I try to incorporate her main interest or activities for the year. The song is unique for her—no one else, so it makes her feel very special as I sing it to her occasionally at bedtime and at other appropriate occasions.

Recorded Birth Announcement When our daughter was born, my husband tape-recorded the telephone calls he made to our relatives and friends with the exciting news. It is still a great blessing to me to replay that tape and hear both his joy and the other party's reaction. When she is older, we plan to share it with our daughter to help her see how thrilled we have always been to have her in our family.

24

Visualizing Usefulness and Achievement

Missionary Mother Our sixth child was born when our oldest child was only eight years old. I was feeling I could never be of any use to the Lord, as all I did was take care of children and their needs. I shared my feelings with my mother-in-law. She told me that if I could raise these six children to love the Lord and want to live for Him, I would have done a missionary's job. This changed my attitude toward myself, my husband, my children, motherhood, and my home. I really began to appreciate the important role of the mother, and it changed my whole life.

Children's Cookbook Our youngest child is often overshadowed by her older brother, who always gets the highest grades and seems to achieve in physical activities as well. At Christmas we found an idea to help her feel very special. An aunt gave her a children's cookbook as a gift. Every week now as I grocery shop, we include ingredients for her to prepare one meal or part of a meal. It's a fun sharing time for us "girls" in the kitchen together. We've all enjoyed some of the new dishes Mom didn't think of trying before.

Stubborn Will   When our son was very young he was very stubborn. Seriously, he did nothing right. He had a very high IQ and was a real frustration to us. He did everything opposite from the way he was told to do it. At night after he fell asleep I would go into his room and tell him how much I loved him, how much God loved him, and ask the Lord for an answer. One night when I went in he was still awake, so I asked him, "David, don't you want Mama to praise you? To tell you that you've done a good job? That you've done it right?" He said, "Yes." I was rather surprised by the sincerity in that one-word answer. So I said, "Then please do something right, Honey, so I can. I really want to, David."

The following day, when he got home from school, he did some yard work I had asked him to do several days earlier. He did it perfectly. God reminded me quickly of what I'd told David the night before. Let me tell you—I praised that boy! I told everyone who came and showed them what a good job he had done. I never had to worry about our yard ever again. From then on he did it beautifully. He even does it occasionally now, when he sees a need, even though he's married with a home of his own. Need I tell you that his own yards and lawns are well kept?